WOMEN IN STEM

KATALIN KARIKÓ
CUTTING-EDGE BIOCHEMIST

by Clara MacCarald

Pogo Books, an imprint of Jump! Library by FlutterBee

Ideas for Parents and Teachers

Pogo Books let children practice reading informational text while introducing them to nonfiction features such as headings, labels, sidebars, maps, and diagrams, as well as a table of contents, glossary, and index.

Carefully leveled text with a strong photo match offers early fluent readers the support they need to succeed.

Before Reading

- "Walk" through the book and point out the various nonfiction features. Ask the student what purpose each feature serves.
- Look at the glossary together. Read and discuss the words.

During Reading

- Have the child read the book independently.
- Invite them to list questions that arise from reading.

After Reading

- Discuss the child's questions. Talk about how they might find answers to those questions.
- Prompt the child to think more. Ask: Have you ever gotten a vaccine? What was it for?

Pogo Books are published by Jump!
3500 American Blvd W, Suite 150
Bloomington, MN 55431
www.jumplibrary.com

Jump! is a division of FlutterBee Education Group.

Library of Congress Cataloging-in-Publication Data

Names: MacCarald, Clara, 1979- author
Title: Katalin Karikó: cutting-edge biochemist by Clara MacCarald.
Description: Bloomington, MN: Jump!, Inc., [2026]
Series: Women in STEM | Includes index.
Audience: Ages 7-10
Identifiers: LCCN 2025028148 (print)
LCCN 2025028149 (ebook)
ISBN 9798896623762 (hardcover)
ISBN 9798896623779 (paperback)
ISBN 9798896623786 (ebook)
Subjects: LCSH: Karikó, Katalin–Juvenile literature
Women biochemists–Biography–Juvenile literature
Biochemists–Biography–Juvenile literature
Hungarian Americans–Biography–Juvenile literature
Classification: LCC QP511.8.K37 M33 2026 (print)
LCC QP511.8.K37 (ebook)
LC record available at https://lccn.loc.gov/2025028148
LC ebook record available at https://lccn.loc.gov/2025028149

Editor: Katie Chanez
Designer: Emma Almgren-Bersie

Photo Credits: Independent Photo Agency Srl/Alamy, cover (foreground); WESTOCK PRODUCTIONS/Shutterstock, cover (vaccine); Christopher Michel/Wikimedia, 1; dra_schwartz/iStock, 3; Sipa USA/Alamy, 4; andreswd/iStock, 6-7; MattL_Images/Shutterstock, 7; Michele Ursi/Shutterstock, 8; years/iStock, 9; fatido/iStock, 9 (inset); Naeblys/iStock, 10-11; Lu ShaoJi/Getty, 12-13; ZUMA Press, Inc./Alamy, 14-15; AnnaStills/Adobe Stock, 16-17; ollo/iStock, 18; Halfpoint/iStock, 19; TT News Agency/Alamy, 20-21; Paramonov Alexander/Shutterstock, 23.

Printed in the United States of America at Corporate Graphics in North Mankato, Minnesota.

TABLE OF CONTENTS

CHAPTER 1

GENE MESSAGES

Katalin Karikó is a **biochemist**. She studies **chemicals** in living things.

Katalin was born in Hungary in 1955. People call her Kati. As a kid, she loved learning. Kati won a science **award** in high school. She went to the **University** of Szeged in 1973.

In 1978, Kati started looking at **genes**. Genes help make us who we are. They decide things like eye and hair color.

Kati was interested in mRNA. mRNA is a chemical. It carries messages from our genes to our **cells**. The messages tell cells how to make **proteins**. Our bodies need proteins to live and grow.

CHAPTER 2

MAKING VACCINES

Scientists could make mRNA in a lab. They could change it to make different proteins. Kati wanted to make mRNA **vaccines**. These would help people.

Some vaccines have dead or weak **microbes** in them. A vaccine teaches the **immune system** what to look for. It learns to destroy the microbes. If they come in again, the immune system can better fight them!

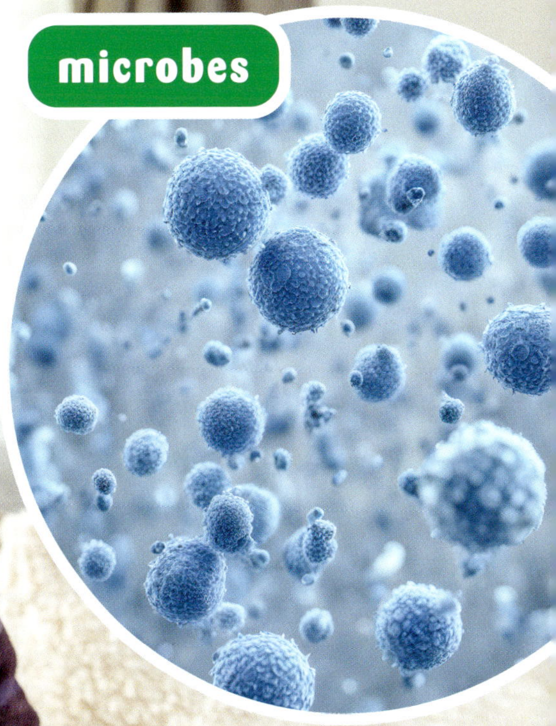

Living microbes in a vaccine can give people the disease the vaccine is supposed to stop. But mRNA vaccines are different. There is no microbe. The vaccine can't give the person the disease. mRNA tells cells to make microbe proteins. The immune system learns to fight this way.

TAKE A LOOK!

How do mRNA vaccines work? Take a look!

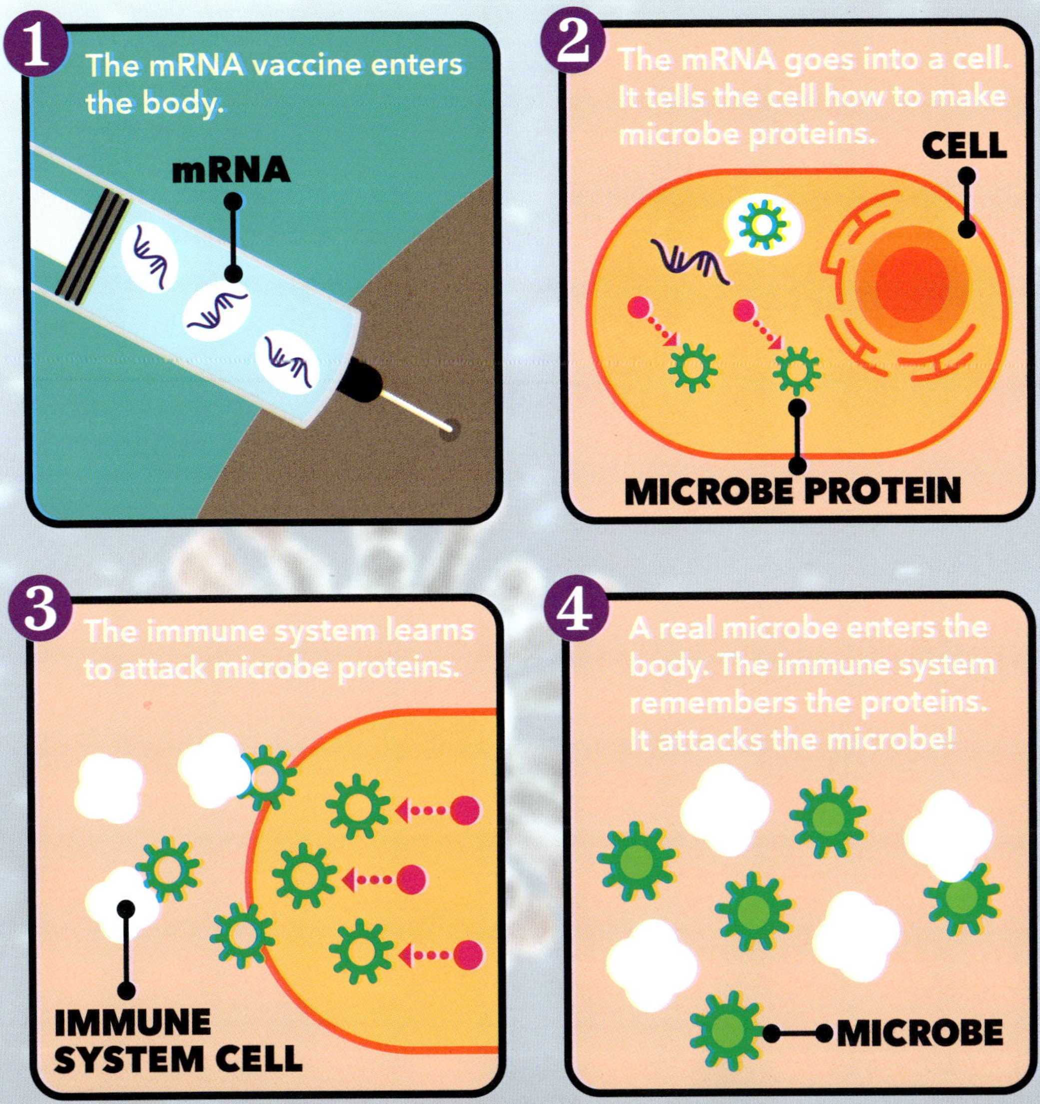

In 1985, Kati moved to the United States. She kept working on mRNA. She studied it in petri dishes.

DID YOU KNOW?

Petri dishes are small. They are see-through. Scientists use them to study how cells grow. They use them to test medicines, too.

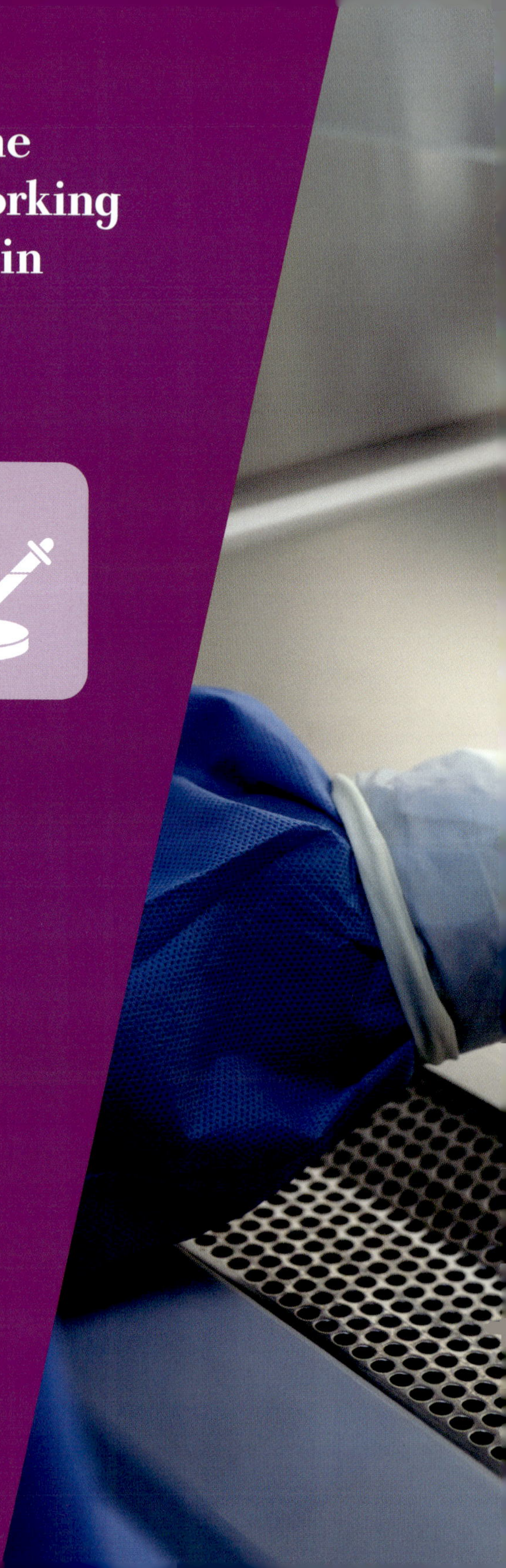

petri dish

Drew
Weissman

Many scientists thought mRNA vaccines wouldn't work. Why? They had tried **injecting** lab mRNA into a mouse. But the mouse's immune system fought it. The mRNA couldn't reach the mouse's cells.

Kati met Drew Weissman in 1997. Drew studied the immune system. Kati and Drew started working together.

DID YOU KNOW?

Scientists don't test new medicines on people right away. Why? It could make them sick. Scientists test medicine in labs or on animals first.

Kati and Drew discovered mRNA from animal cells had a special **code**. In 2005, they found a way to copy that code. They added it to lab mRNA. The immune system didn't attack this mRNA. It worked!

They also made a way to get mRNA safely to cells. How? They used tiny drops of fat. Fat coats the mRNA. The body doesn't break it down. People had a way to use this new mRNA!

vaccine

CHAPTER 3

FIGHTING COVID-19

Kati and Drew had made a huge discovery! By 2010, companies were using their method to try to make mRNA vaccines. Kati worked at one. It was called BioNTech.

BioNTech headquarters, Germany

In 2019, a virus started spreading across the world. It caused an illness. It was called COVID-19. Millions of people died.

Nobel Prize

Scientists raced to make vaccines. Some made mRNA vaccines. They couldn't have done it without Kati's work. Billions of people got COVID-19 vaccines. The vaccines saved 17 million lives in one year!

Kati and Drew received a **Nobel Prize** in 2023. Their work had helped the world! Kati still works on mRNA. She hopes to find new ways to keep people healthy.

DID YOU KNOW?

Vaccines can take up to 15 years to make. BioNTech and Pfizer worked together. They made an mRNA COVID-19 vaccine in nine months!

ACTIVITIES & TOOLS

TRY THIS!

MATCHING MICROBES

See how vaccines help the immune system with this fun activity!

What You Need:

- 16 index cards
- crayons, markers, or colored pencils
- timer or other way to keep time
- two people

1. Draw a circle in the middle of 12 of the index cards. These will be microbes.
2. On three microbe cards, draw small triangles around the circle. On the next three microbe cards, draw small squares around the circle. On the next three, draw small circles around the large circle. On the last three, draw Xs around the circle.
3. There should be four blank cards left. Draw a triangle on one. Draw a square on another. Then draw a circle on the next card. Put an X on the last one. These are vaccines.
4. Mix up the microbe cards. Put them face down in front of one person. That person will be the immune system.
5. Choose one of the vaccine cards. Show the card to the player for five seconds. This is the shape the player needs to look for. Set the card face down.
6. Set the timer. Have the player find the microbes with the shape that was on the vaccine card. How long does it take the immune system to get them all?

GLOSSARY

award: A prize or honor for accomplishing something.

biochemist: A scientist who studies chemicals found in living things.

cells: The smallest units of living things.

chemicals: Substances that have specific characteristics and can interact with other chemicals to change form.

code: A system used to send messages or store information.

genes: Parts of chromosomes that are passed from parents to children and determine how a person looks and grows.

immune system: The system that protects the body against disease.

injecting: Putting medicine into a body through a needle.

microbes: Extremely small living things that cause disease.

Nobel Prize: A special award given to someone who does important things for the world.

proteins: Chemicals found in all living cells that are necessary for life.

university: A place where people study for degrees beyond high school.

vaccines: Drugs that protect people or animals from certain diseases.

Nobel Prize

INDEX

TO LEARN MORE

Finding more information is as easy as 1, 2, 3.

1. Go to www.factsurfer.com
2. Enter "Katalin Kariko" into the search box.
3. Choose your book to see a list of websites.

FACT SURFER